And So I Think

A JOURNEY into my thoughts

2nd Edition

Brian E. Stevens, Sr., MSHCM, ADRMC, DDIC

And So I Think

A JOURNEY into my thoughts

2nd Edition

Brian E. Stevens

Description:

Take a journey into my thoughts. You will experience quotes & thoughts on spiritual matters, leadership, relationships, and some humorous jargon based upon sleep deprivation. I am sure you will be entertained and most of all, INSPIRED. Enjoy!

Special discounts on bulk quantities are available to corporations, professional associations, nonprofits, and other organizations. For details, contact the Information Department, N2B Solutions Group, Inc.: info@n2bsolutionsgroup.com.

N2B Solutions Group, Inc., 10730 Potranco Road, San Antonio, Texas 78251

Website: www.n2bsolutionsgroup.com - Book Sale

This publication is designed to provide authoritative opinions in regard to the thoughts of the Author. It is sold with the understanding that the publisher is not engaged in rendering legal, accounting, or other professional service. If legal advice or other expert assistance is required, the services of a competent professional should be sought.

Copyright @ 2013 by Brian E. Stevens, Sr.
All rights reserved.
Printed in the United States of America.

This publication may not be reproduced, stored in a retrieval system, or transmitted in whole or in part, in any form or by any means, electronic, mechanical, photocopying, recording, or otherwise, without the prior written permission of the author.

ISBN-13: 978-0615640921
ISBN-10: 0615640923

Acknowledgments: This is dedicated to my friends and family, especially my kids who kept me up all hours of the night so that I may write due to sleep deprivation. To my dear friends and acquaintances, thank you for encouraging me to stop posting my thoughts on the internet and actually place them within a book. Well this one's for you guys. To the one I continuously travel the road which is straighter than the straightest of lines, thank you for your love and motivation. As Chief Operating Officer at Business Investment Growth, Inc. (BiGAUSTIN), www.big.org, they give me inspiration on a daily bases.

CONTENTS

Experience..................................5

Spiritual....................................8

Love..19

Relationships............................28

Leadership...............................32

Humorous.................................37

Thoughts..................................43

Life..52

Self-Improvement......................57

EXPERIENCE

When you relive the PAST, be prepared to open the pain that goes along with it, but when you live for the PRESENT, the gifts are much better.

****

The best way to forget the past is creating a better future.

****

WHEN YOU SELLOUT YOUR LOVED ONES WITH HALF TRUTHS, PLEASE MAKE SURE THE DEVIL GIVES YOU A RECEIPT!

I had rather be stabbed in the back by a close friend than stabbed in the front by a family member. It is easier to recover from a wound to the back than a direct strike to the heart.

* * * * * * * * *

When you feel all is lost, it is ok. You now have the ability to allow new and improved things to happen within your life. Close the doors of the past in order to step through new ones.

* * * * * * * * *

Closed eye makes the heart heal faster. Meaning: It's harder to get over someone if you're constantly looking at old photos, videos, and letters.

Happiness over wealth makes for a joyous life.

* * * * * * * * *

Sometimes pain comes from making the right decisions in the short term in order for you to receive lifelong happiness in the long term.

* * * * * * * * *

I have learned firsthand that material things don't buy you joy, happiness, or peace of mind. It does buy you a bunch of stuff; Choose peace of mind, you will have less STUFF to get rid of at the end of the day.

SPIRITUAL

Love is consistent. Humans are not. Why consistently complain that someone does not love you? Love yourself well enough to let go and let God! Simple spiritual logic.

* * * * * * * * *

Each day brings new opportunities. Never allow someone to talk you out of your blessings.

* * * * * * * * *

A fool will discard Gods worldly blessings on his quest to rule the universe. PRIDE

Stop taking the easy way out. Stop being co-dependent on someone else's success. You don't deserve a hand out, you deserve blessings. You're a child of God with power, inner and outer beauty, and a vast wealth of resources that only God can supply. But here's the thing, you must do more than just ask him for help. You must believe.

****

God does not reward those who do evil. You may think he does by looking at someone who has achieved a level of financial means, but external visuals do not allow you to witness their internal heartache.

If you put more thought in what you wear to the club every weekend than you do on how you are going to serve the Lord, don't be surprised when you get to Heaven and God gives you a drink ticket and VIP passes to club "I'd Be Damned."

* * * * * * * * *

Don't ever apologize for making decisions based upon how the Lord wants you to live. True, some may not like your decision, but it's best to be temporarily upset than to be eternally dammed.

* * * * * * * * *

Fear and insecurities will blind you from achieving all you were created to be. Spiritual maturity is knowing when to say, **"ENOUGH IS ENOUGH"** then handing your battles over to our Lord and Savior.

As I lay here, I think back to the Bible where Jesus was tempted by the accuser. He was offered power, kingdoms, and riches. Jesus chose the correct door which led him back to Heaven. What door would you choose? Are you being tempted? What would I choose? Am I being tempted? Is it going to be earthly STUFF or the kingdom of Heaven? Use the one and only life line that counts. God's line.

* * * * * * * * *

Family gives us energy, either positive or negative, they still and will always be family. Now, if you choose to go over for Christmas, may I suggest bringing an old fruitcake that was featured in the Last Super. Let go of the PAST by practicing forgiveness. By doing so, you will open doors of joy, peace, and serenity.

The accuser shall not win this war even though he has won a lot of battles in your life. Choose God and eternal life. The spotlight of non-importance is just that, not important. Who does it really benefit when earthly light ceases to shine on you and your circle of followers? Please take door number one for eternal life. A better view for the price.

* * * * * * * * *

Even though you see their smile, you may never see their pain. A simple hello can save a life. Think about it. Everyone you say hello to is a person who could have been contemplating ending it all because of feeling unnoticed and or unwanted. I choose not to have that guilt upon my shoulders, so I've decided to say hello in order to save a life. Will you accept God's challenge today?

Workouts are not just good for the body but for the soul. Yes the soul needs to be worked out by increasing your faith. Read the bible like you hit the gym. It's sword to shield as weights to muscle gain.

* * * * * * * *

Ask and God will show you the light even if you prefer walking in the dark.

* * * * * * * * *

God doesn't bring all relationships together. He allows you to make comparisons between the old, new, good, and bad. More importantly, what your future in-laws will like.

God said to me, "A stone or a mountain?" I then asked what did he mean? He replied, "What is heavier, a stone or a mountain?" I had answered by saying, "Why a stone, Father." His last words to me were, "Then why do you continuously attempt to carry the weight of the mountain when I had answered your prayers, took care of your problems, and reduced them a stone?"

LESSON LEARNED:

God knows I am aggressive. Mountains attract me because they seem like a challenge. When I get over my head, God ALWAYS reveals where I need to be. He shows me what is good and what is not so good for me. He is talking to you, as well, but turndown the extra noise in your life so that you may hear him more clearly. I hear you loud and clear Father. Thank you.

As I lay here counting my blessings, it just hit me, I ran out of numbers.

* * * * * * * *

Letting go at times may be the hardest thing you will ever have to do. Put your trust and faith in God, he will reveal the positives and negatives in order to make the healing go smoother.

* * * * * * * * *

I AM ONLY BECAUSE GOD ALLOWS ME TO BE!

Change the way you see your current situation and know that you are exactly where God wants you to be. You just have to believe it.

* * * * * * * * *

Even public opinion could not stop Jesus from entering Heaven. Ole ye of so little faith.

* * * * * * * * *

Those who say, "He or she thinks they are better than everyone." They are saying this because internally, they feel as if you ARE better than them. Pray for them Saints.

Not all smiling teeth are happy for you. Do not be fooled. The accuser also knows your wants and needs. Be mindful and pray before making any decisions in your life. It had taken me years to finally figure that out and I'm still learning every day.

* * * * * * * * *

I challenge you to stop doing the accusers work. Example: In my opinion, the accuser came up with the Slogan, "Promises were made to be broken." Think about it. God said that He promises to never leave us. So with that being said, who do you believe that promises are made to be broken, God or the accuser? Once all lies and excuses are exposed, true healing can begin.

* * * * * * * * *

The fog of confusion is lifted through prayer.

The wise embrace change while the fool sees it as a failure. Accept your blessings with opened arms, not folded ones.

* * * * * * * * *

Mom use to tell me that only a fool would take financial advice from broke people or relationship advice from those unable to sustain them. Be careful of those who proclaim to be advisors of wisdom within your camp. The blind leading the blind only leads to devastation but through prayer, all things can be achieved.

* * * * * * * * *

Never give up on the weak, for God is the weight which makes us strong. The best part is, you don't need a gym membership.

LOVE

No one ever promised love would be a garden of roses, unless it is showered with the light of faith, air of passion, and sprinkled with water of sincerity. Love is to be embraced, not made an enemy.

* * * * * * * * *

You don't need power, glory, fortune, or fame. You don't even need reservations at a fancy restaurant or a spotlight announcing your arrival. All you need is love which truly enriches the soul. That's all that matters in life, LOVE, TRUE LOVE.

* * * * * * * * *

When climbing a tree to get to the top doesn't mean you'll touch every branch. Love is the same way, meaning loving another maybe different than how you loved someone else in the past. Just as a tree is still a tree, love is still love, as long as you do whatever it takes to make it to the top.

Most people ask the question, "Do you love me?" That is the wrong question to ask. The correct question is, "Tell me, what does love means to you?" Behavioral change begins by asking the right questions in order for you to start understanding what life is all about.

* * * * * * * *

Love is offering to cook you a nice romantic dinner. Lust is offering you a can of soup with no can opener.

* * * * * * * * *

TEST OF TRUE LOVE: WHEN THEY HURT, YOU HURT.

True love is sought through actions and not through words alone. Food may look good on the plate but won't do you any good unless eaten.

* * * * * * * * *

If asked how deep, how far, and how wide is my love? You must first travel past Mars then make a right at Venus. From there a slight turn at Pluto. Once you have completed this, continue your journey and make up names for every planet you then encounter until God calls you home. I can hear my ex now, "Well you must have gotten lost after I said, "I DO!"

* * * * * * * * *

Love requires action and not just the movement of the mouth.

The good thing about being in love, is being in love with someone who gets what being in love is all about. They learn your habits inside and out, and still chooses to stick around. Cheers to new beginnings and seal closed doors with padlocks.

* * * * * * * * *

Hold on to true love and not just past memories. Love is the only thing that surpasses death.

* * * * * * * * *

When true love is involved, the weight on one's shoulder becomes divided because of a beautiful smile. Lifelong relationships are real. If you happen to be in one, embrace your blessing every day with a simple, "Good morning gorgeous." It would mean the world to her/him.

The fundamental difference between LOVE and LUST is: LOVE is simple and smooth. LUST is complex and forced. Learn the difference between the two before you wake up stuck in the Matrix, while he continues to take the BLUE PILL!

* * * * * * * * *

Love always creates, it never destroys.

* * * * * * * * *

Stop looking for someone who reminds you of an old love. Just like a copier machine, it does not matter the quality or richness of the paper, it will never be the original, but a copy.

Love is like a job. The harder you work at it, the greater the rewards.

* * * * * * * * *

Love is truly a WORK in progress, some would just rather stay UNEMPLOYED.

* * * * * * * * *

Love can be transferable. Love can be co-signed. With that being said, love could also be repossessed.

Love isn't supposed to equal hurt. If it does, you may need to redefine the true meaning of love. On the flip side, if you have found true love, embrace it and do whatever it takes to keep the passion burning within it like a wild fire. Complacency is the enemy of fulfillment.

* * * * * * * * *

Do not be the one who lies in order to love. Be the one that loves in order not to lie. **Key take away:** Just be you and if you aren't accepted then it wasn't meant to be in the first place. You are perfect and special in your own way. If you do not believe that, well at least you got a free dinner out of the deal.

* * * * * * * * *

The only time it hurts when wearing your heart on your sleeve, is when your shirt just happens to be sleeveless.

Love isn't to be fought for. If it was meant to be it would be. If there is something standing in the way and causing problems within your relationship, it's not because of love, it is because someone within your relationship is allowing it to happen, thus not putting a stop to it. Even a fool can only hold the job as a fool for so long, before their services are no longer needed.

* * * * * * * * *

"Oh she loves me. Let me count the ways!" Starting with -6, -5, -4.....

* * * * * * * * *

Love is like a water well. If not used, it too will become dry and useless.

At times, being invisible has its advantages and disadvantages. The advantage is you can go through life without being seen and or getting hurt. The disadvantage is you can go through life without experiencing love or a gentle kiss.

* * * * * * * * *

Some people's priority is all about the interest made from their bank account. The ONLY interest that should matter is the love received from your children. That investment far exceeds monetary gain. It's sad that some are so lost in the fog that they truly miss this simple concept.

RELATIONSHIPS

It is not that your man's too manly to love you. It may be that your self-esteem is too low to know the difference.

* * * * * * * * *

If you think those who make empty promises are your everything, then you've never required much in the first place.

* * * * * * * * *

Like I have always said, "It's not that you will miss a good thing until it's gone. Oh no, never that! It's the fact that you thought that good thing would never leave."

Do not be so independent you talk yourself out of a relationship with a possible soul mate. Loneliness is not an option for those deserving of true happiness.

* * * * * * * * *

When she needed me most, I gave her less. Immaturity v. Manhood.

* * * * * * * * *

The fastest way to a woman's heart is through YOUR ears.

Sometimes letting go can position you for a bigger catch. Be wise and think with your brain and not with your heart since the **HEART** can be **ATTACKED** - Heart Attack - Get it?

* * * * * * * * *

Set relationship standards so that the next time around, instead of bringing something to the table, how about just building one together.

* * * * * * * * *

Don't elect someone as your King or Queen if they are not worthy of ROYALTY!

If you find yourself in a relationship and you argue so much that your new excuse is, "Oh this is just how we communicate!" It just may be time to practice the art of being silent so you may BOTH HEAR one another.

* * * * * * * * *

Do you consider yourself a relationship hoarder? Clean sweep your thought process and close the door forever. When doors are left opened, a lot of energy will be lost.

* * * * * * * * * * * *

Sometimes it's best to cut all loses and start fresh where no one knows your name or credit score.

Never go to bed hot tempered because when you awake, it may not just be your attitude that is ON FIRE!

* * * * * * * * *

What's awesome about being a power couple is maintaining that power even when the lights are off or on.

LEADERSHIP

The only DEFEAT I recognize are the ones connected to my body that strikes the ground with every step forward I take. Failure is a choice, not an option, and I CHOOSE NOT TO FAIL!

In life, every battle makes you more prepared for the wars of setbacks. There's strength in being proactive and forecasting.

* * * * * * * * *

True test of leadership is measured by how well you manage your home.

* * * * * * * * *

Key to success: Find out what everyone else is doing and you do the opposite. There is no fun being average when you are born for greatness.

One who masters the power of influence master the art of job stability.

* * * * * * * * *

If you truly led from the front, you wouldn't worry about who's got your back.

* * * * * * * * *

Is your determination as strong as you're talking about achieving it? Always remember, two steps forward can win marathons.

Do not depend on others for your own success. That is your job and yours alone. Don't allow anyone to tell you're not smart enough to make things happen. Success is what you make it. Success is also how YOU define it, not them.

* * * * * * * * *

Comfort is the enemy of progression.

* * * * * * * * *

The key to success is knowing the difference between Leadership and Management. Management is a position. Leadership influences others to effectively get the job done proactively. So, is there a MANAGER or a LEADER in your midst?

Make today a blessing to those around you. Do not overkill them with kindness, just be kind. Did you know that those who smile more at work typically get promoted faster than those who don't? It's true. If you don't believe me, just ask the person you're training right now!

* * * * * * * *

The less you talk; the less you will be noticed. The less you will be noticed; the less you will become successful in business. Key principle to owning anything successful is, TALKING about it.

* * * * * * * *

If you are the type that always waits for someone to make the first move, then competition is thanking you right now. Those who sleep on opportunities typically wakes up alone and unemployed.

HUMOR

Since when did parents become scared of their kids? If I had ever cursed at my mom, the next thing would be Jesus saying, **"WELCOME MY SON. I TOLD YOU TO DUCK!"** "Heck Lord, I thought you were talking about what I should make for dinner!"

* * * * * * * * *

Treadmill Observation: This kid is talking back to his mother like HE gave birth to HER. I love my kids to death, but you best believe I tell them, **"YOU'RE NOT A CHIROPRACTOR SO SAVE THE BACK TALK TO THE EXPERTS!"**

I can tell a man came up with this statement: **"No pain. No gain."** Well, here is what I say about that. Give HIM an epidural but **NOT THE FIRST TRY EPIDURAL.** The 2nd or 3rd try epidural, then look him in his face and scream out loud for all women in the world, **"NO PAIN NO GAIN HUH MR. SPORTS MANNNNN!!!!"**

* * * * * * * * *

She'll suggest you work out when you're pudgy, but will ask, "WHO ARE YOU TRYING TO IMPRESS?" when she starts noticing the results.

* * * * * * * * *

Money may buy you the world, but it can never purchase the one important thing, a personality!

Unconditional love with conditions is like selling your car to purchase gas, it makes no sense.

* * * * * * * * *

They say, "Life is a box of ……" Well what if you just happen to be a diabetic? Who comes up with this stuff?

* * * * * * * * *

I only pray to continue to be the fountain of love from which quenches your thirst, every drop promising eternal passion, as the days are long and the nights are even longer. Our love is equaled to the straightest of lines. It is that line, I shall walk and never tire. I call this poem, MAN CAVE!

Whoever said, "Money can't buy you love," MUST HAVE NEVER PURCHASED AN EXPENSIVE YORKIE FOR THEIR KIDS!

* * * * * * * * *

Even in light of ignorance and injustice, there is still light. Never give up; hope is just around the corner. Let's just pray your ex-wife is not named Hope!

* * * * * * * * *

Have you ever met people so bitter they make lemons jealous? Add some spice to your life because at the end of the day, it's your life.

Yes ladies, even some men have full body pillows. We'll just hide it when you come over.

* * * * * * * * *

Yes, your ships have came in plenty of times. Too bad they've all been TUG boats.

* * * * * * * * *

God says, "Ye without sin cast the first stone!" Brian says, "Ye who missed this message must have been out on a smoke break!"

"OH I AM A CHRISTIAN. I DON'T CARE IF YOU BELIEVE ME OR NOT. I GO TO CHURCH EVERY SUNDAY. IF YOU DON'T BELIEVE ME, JUST ASK MY VOO DOO DOLL. HE'LL VOUCH FOR ME!" Some people are lost in the midst of the fog.

* * * * * * * * *

If your soul and integrity is for sale, I pray the check doesn't bounce!

* * * * * * * * *

What ever happened to ONE NATION UNDER GOD? I'm pretty sure our creator is bi-partisan.

THOUGHTS

Ignorance is like a rash. No matter what you do, it will still get under your skin.

* * * * * * * * *

Those who throw rocks may not be aware of the **BOULDERS** rolling behind them.

* * * * * * * * *

If you treat those at work better than those at home, it may be wise to bring work home. **PRIORITIES.**

Conflict only grows when watered with attention.

* * * * * * * * *

When opportunity calls, the wise jump for joy while the fool asks to take a message.

* * * * * * * * *

Don't focus on making the right or wrong choice. At the end the day, a choice still needs to be made.

It's better to focus on the big picture instead of short-term gratifications.

* * * * * * * * *

Even fool's gold shines and yet holds no value, but only to the fool who tries to sell it.

* * * * * * * * *

Beware of those who offer ways to construct a boat rather than lend a hand to prevent you from drowning.

You'll never be happy searching for what has already been found.

* * * * * * * * *

Success is a trip in which you will encounter many different roads. Travel smartly, travel wisely, but most of all TRAVEL!!!!

* * * * * * * * *

At times it maybe a Theraflu kind of day, but what makes it ok, is when they ask, "How can I make it better?"

Beauty is in the eyes of the beholder, but food sustains life and prosperity. Choices

* * * * * * * * *

Have you ever wanted to wake up in order to truly WAKE UP?

* * * * * * * * *

The heart can see what is invisible to the eye even in darkness.

The fundamental difference between a fool and a wise man is when the fool professes to know everything, the wise man nods.

* * * * * * * * *

Family: Protect them more than you would a bank account only because the interest is greater and longer lasting.

* * * * * * * * *

Do not allow footprints towards success be covered by your betrayal. The pathway back home may be so hard to find let alone, non-existent.

It's not that people are judging you as a person. It's the words coming from your mouth that are being judged.

* * * * * * * * *

When you believe something is truly solid, best believe it can be made into liquid depending on how hot the situation gets.

* * * * * * * * *

Some people have a Pilates type of faith. TWISTED!

The chaser wouldn't have to chase if they truly understood their self worth.

* * * * * * * * *

We make time for things we want and excuses for things we don't want.

* * * * * * * * *

Famous, in my opinion, is defined by the millions of men and women, who have picked up a weapon in defense of our great and wonderful United States of America.

In today's economy, middle class really means back of the class. Lower class means you can't even get into the class room. They say change is on the rise. It must be in the form of unemployment. Come on America. We can make this work if we all work together.

* * * * * * * * *

Drama doesn't attracted people. People attract drama. Be the bigger person by repelling ignorance. It does wonders for the soul.

LIFE

The rabbit never sees how close it is to the cliff while in the fog, but the turtle does.

Lesson learned: Don't be in such a rush. Fall this time, you may never recover.

* * * * * * * * *

Reality always has a way of clearing out the fog in your life in order for the view to be clearer.

* * * * * * * * *

Working out is more than a choice but a lifestyle. Healthy living for 20XX and beyond.

Life changes with a simple thought followed by a decision, followed by action. With that being said, set your ACTion in motion!

* * * * * * * * *

GACAL = GIVEN ANOTHER CHANGE AT LIFE. Don't waste it, make every day count like it's your last because it just may be your last.

* * * * * * * * *

Let change begin. Happiness is priceless. Family is everything.

It is a natural part of life to have a somber kind of day once in a while. You are human you know.

Life is all about the choices we make. Each choice has a learning point. Don't be that doormat for someone who feels entitled to walk all over you. There is way more fish in the sea, but you need to stop fishing at the local lake!

* * * * * * * * *

Accept failure as a natural form of self development. Once you have mastered it, change your thought process and embrace the sweet taste of success. Failure allows you to come up with a different plan of action. This process is called, LIFE CHANGE.

Life was made to be set in motion with death being the brakes.

* * * * * * * * *

Making no decision is making a decision. Life lesson.

* * * * * * * * *

A diamond cannot be a diamond without pressure.

* * * * * * * * *

We are born to die but how many of us truly live? Look at your life. Average is not part of Gods plan for you. Start fresh. Start new. Start living NOW.

The most pivotal part of reaching maximum maturity is reflecting on your past and saying, "Wow What The Heck Was I Thinking?"

* * * * * * * * *

Good or bad, nothing truly leaves your life without teaching you SOMETHING.

* * * * * * * * *

Embrace your struggles. It does not matter if you lose or win. Attempt to strive for something better than the norm. That is life's challenge.

SELF IMPROVEMENT

The worst thing you can do to your heart is lie to it. Change comes from within and no matter how you try to hide your true feelings, fate has a way of making everything come to light soon enough.

* * * * * * * * *

Today's ownership day. Evaluate what makes you happy and purge anything that doesn't. It is far better to lose weight than to lose your mind!

* * * * * * * *

Educate your mind and the rest shall follow. Ignorance is so underrated and yet so over achieved.

Winners don't chase money; money chases them. Find happiness outside a paycheck. Life's too short to be rich, unhappy, but well dressed.

* * * * * * * * *

Accept **PRESSURE** whenever you are faced with adversity. It is true that **PRESSURE** burst pipes, but **PRESSURE** also make **DIAMONDS**. It is all about how you look at things. Success comes in many different forms if you don't allow **PRESSURE** to **BURST YOUR SPIRIT**.

* * * * * * * * *

MIND RIGHT + BODY TIGHT = SUCCESS IN SIGHT.

Don't fight 10 rounds with someone only to realize, all these years you have been in the wrong ring. Happiness is a choice and so is rebuilding your self-esteem. You can do it. I believe in you.

* * * * * * * * *

Once you realize self worth, then and only then, will your options become abundant.

* * * * * * * * *

Procrastination is like bad credit and unwanted house guest; it really isn't going anywhere unless you decide to do something about it.

Working out is an awesome way to release stress. 20 to 30 minutes of doing something physical will make a world of difference.

* * * * * * * * *

Sometimes what we think is not what we thought. Best course of action? Stop thinking and just do it.

* * * * * * * * *

This is your year for change. No excuses for selfishness.

Low self-esteem can be dreadful. Increasing self-worth is the fastest way to a full body and soul makeover.

* * * * * * * * *

True happiness needs to be found from within before found in others.

* * * * * * * * *

Healing begins when you acknowledge you need to be healed. Pain is real but temporary.

It is good to have wants and needs, but best to have encouragement.

* * * * * * * * *

Increase your self-esteem because you truly are beautiful. I know because your mirror told me so.

* * * * * * * * *

Dreams are continuous and so should your goals in accomplishing them.

If you do not know their story, please do not try and rewrite their book. Just like makeup, it really does not state who the person truly is underneath it all.

* * * * * * * * *

The question is not if you possess enough talent. The correct question is: "How much of your talents is currently being used?"

* * * * * * * * *

It is ok to be a strong woman, but do not be so strong that your outer appearance is stronger than your heart.

Stop worrying about what others have or don't have and take ownership in creating your own success. Pull up your OWN BOOT STRAPS! WHY? BECAUSE AT THE END OF THE DAY, THEY'RE YOUR DARN BOOTS AREN'T THEY?

* * * * * * * * *

It amazes me how people are still trying to live like the Jones'. Little do they know, Mrs. Jones is sleeping with Larry. Larry is sleeping with Mrs. Roberts. Mrs. Roberts just filed bankruptcy, and her dog's a Kibbles & Bits junkie looking for the invisible train wagon.

Summary: What may look good on the outside may not show the chaos going on, on the inside. Be an original. It's cheaper that way.

www.ingramcontent.com/pod-product-compliance
Lightning Source LLC
Chambersburg PA
CBHW060429050426
42449CB00009B/2202